Published by Evans Brothers Limited
2A Portman Mansions
Chiltern Street
London W1U 6NR

© Evans Brothers Limited 2004

First published 2004

Printed in China

British Library Cataloguing in Publication data.

Powell, Jillian
Sam uses a wheelchair. - (Like Me, Like You)
1. Paraplegia - Juvenile literature 2. Paraplegics - Juvenile literature - 3. Wheelchairs - Juvenile literature
I. Title
618.9'209758

ISBN 0237526638

Acknowledgements

The author and publishers would like to thank the following for their help with this book:

Sam, Kathryn and Therese Lawton and Hannah and Kate Clayton.

Thanks also to the Association of Wheelchair Children for their help in the preparation of this book.

All photographs by Gareth Boden

Credits

Series Editor: Louise John
Editor: Julia Bird
Designer: Mark Holt
Production: Jenny Mulvanny

Association of
Wheelchair Children

LIKE ME LIKE YOU

Sam uses a
WHEELCHAIR

JILLIAN POWELL

Evans

Hi, my name is Sam and I use a wheelchair. I live at home with Mum and Dad, my brothers Chris and Michael and my sister Kathryn. We have two pet cats called Ollie and Jazzie.

I have **spina bifida**. It means I don't feel anything below my waist, so I have to be careful not to knock or hurt myself. I can't stand or walk easily so I use a wheelchair to get around. This is the chair I use for school and for days out.

SPINA BIFIDA

A baby born with spina bifida has a backbone that doesn't join up properly.

I share a bedroom with my sister. We get on well with each other. Sometimes Kathryn gets into one of my wheelchairs and we play games, pushing ourselves around and chasing each other.

I have my own bathroom that's easy for me to use. I can push my chair under the basin to wash my face and clean my teeth. I use a special shower chair when I want to have a shower.

In the morning, I have to do some stretching exercises. I do these twice a day and sometimes in PE at school too. Mum helps me by gently stretching my legs and feet. This helps them to grow straight.

Then I put on my **splints**. I wear them all day, except when I'm doing sports. They help to keep my legs and feet in place. I like wearing splints in bright colours! I have to wear special shoes with them, but they're nice shoes so I don't mind too much.

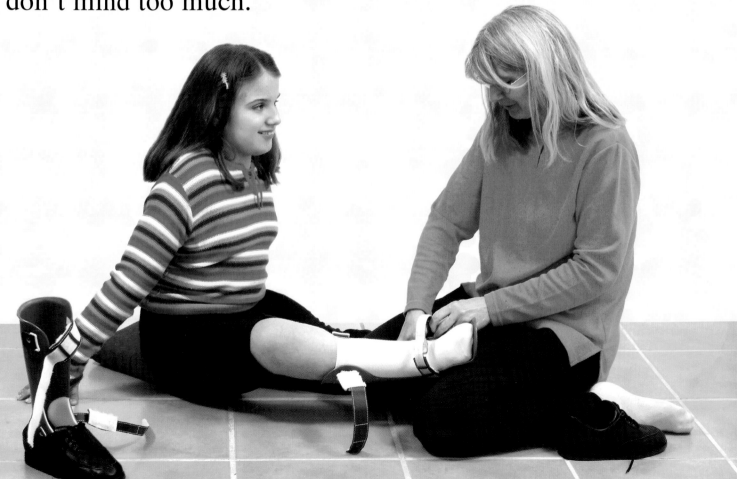

I use this lift when I want to go downstairs. It goes straight from our bedroom to the kitchen. I like reading in the lift and sometimes I'm so busy reading, I forget to get out!

Today, my friend Hannah has come over to spend the day with me. She likes having a ride in the lift too.

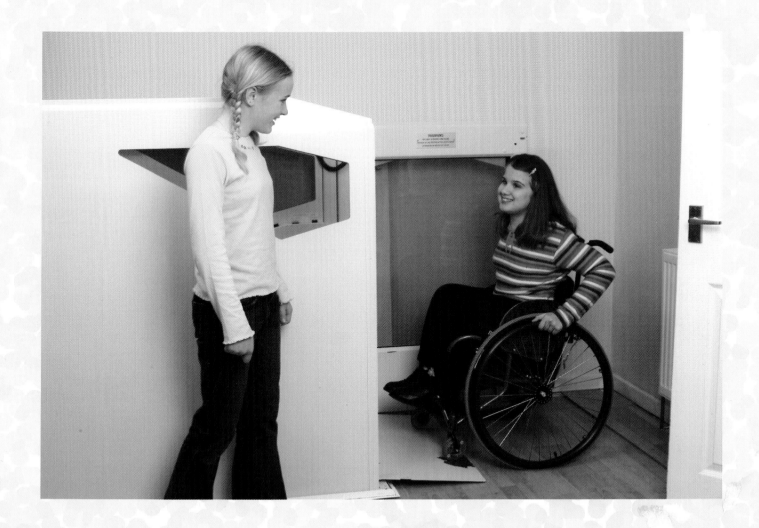

Hannah's coming to the park to watch me practise my wheelchair racing. I go racing once a fortnight. It's one of my favourite sports. I wheel myself down the **ramp** outside our house. Ramps make it much easier for me to get around.

Hannah helps Mum get my wheelchair into the car. I have a special wheelchair for racing. It's very light and fast and it has three wheels. I wear a racing helmet and gloves too.

It's great fun wheelchair racing, and it helps keep my arms strong. I try to practise every week. Hannah has a stop watch so she can time me. I try to go a bit faster each time. Hannah tells me I'm three seconds faster than last time!

Sometimes I enter competitions where I race against other girls and boys in wheelchairs. I show Hannah the medals I've won for coming first in three different races.

After the park, Mum takes me and Hannah to a youth club where we do arts and crafts and sometimes sports. We always have a great time and it's a good place to make new friends.

Sometimes we do baking at the club, too. Today, Hannah and I are making cheese and tomato pizzas. I'm putting lots of cheese on mine!

There's a special toilet at the club that's easy for me to use. It has a wide doorway so I can wheel my chair through easily. There are rails for me to hold on to to lift myself on and off the toilet.

Later on, we play a game of table tennis with some friends. The table has high sides that stop the ball falling on to the floor so I don't have to keep picking it up!

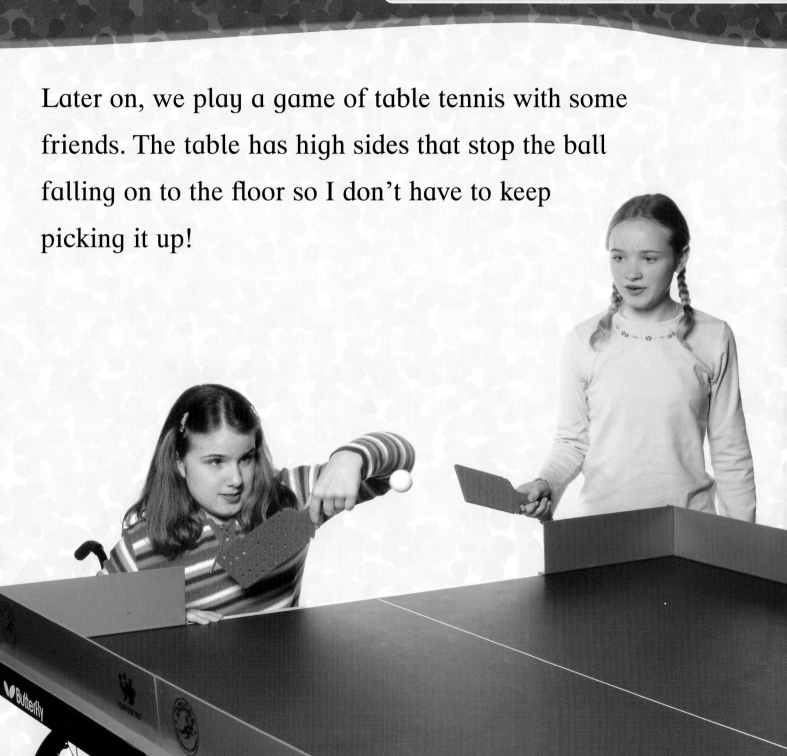

We can do lots of other sports at the club. I like playing basketball. The goal is set low on the wall so that I can reach it more easily.

Sometimes we play a computer dance game. The screen shows you where to put your feet on the dance mats. Hannah has to be quick with her feet! I can follow the dance on the Play Station. I have to be quick with my fingers!

Later, Hannah comes back to my house and we look at some holiday photographs. I often use this standing frame when I'm at home. It helps make my legs stronger. I push a button and the frame lifts me up, then I stand for about an hour.

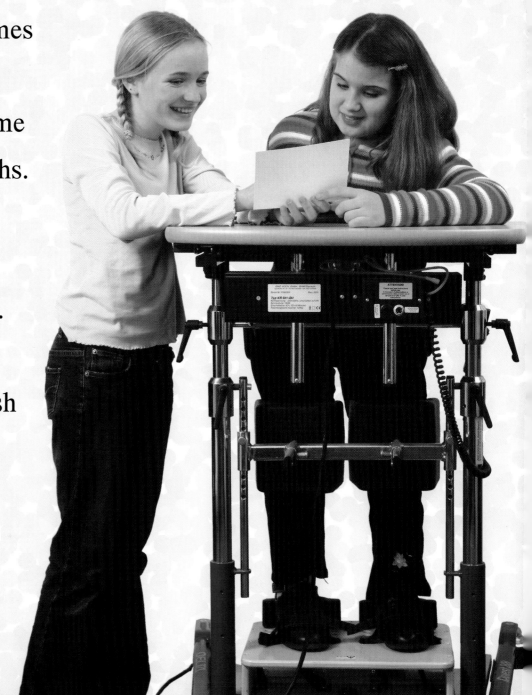

24

It's time for Hannah to go home now. She says goodbye to me, Mum and Ollie.

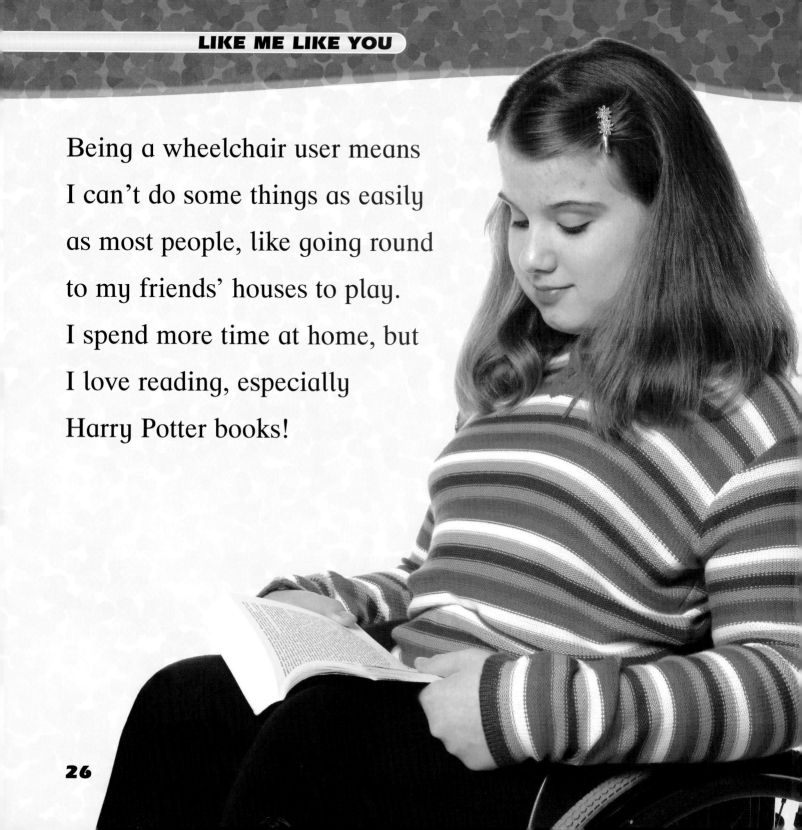

Being a wheelchair user means
I can't do some things as easily
as most people, like going round
to my friends' houses to play.
I spend more time at home, but
I love reading, especially
Harry Potter books!

26

There are lots of sports I can do that are fun too, like basketball. I can join in and play with my friends.

Some people need to use wheelchairs because they are born with a disability, like spina bifida or **cerebral palsy**. Others need to use a wheelchair after they have had an accident or illness.

27

Glossary

Cerebral palsy a condition in which the part of the brain that controls movement is damaged

Ramp a slope in place of steps

Spina bifida a condition in which a baby's backbone does not join up properly before it is born

Splint a hard case which supports and protects parts of the body

Index

Further Information

UNITED KINGDOM
The Association of Wheelchair Children
Tel: 0870 121 0050
www.wheelchairchildren.org.uk
Lots of information for children who are
wheelchair users and their families.

Whizz-Kidz
Tel: 0207 233 6600
www.whizz-kidz.org.uk
A charity that raises money to provide
wheelchairs for children and offers advice,
information and help for them and their families.

British Wheelchair Sports Foundation
www.britishwheelchairsports.org
Information on all kinds of wheelchair sports,
plus disabled camps and events.

AUSTRALIA
Association for Children with a Disability
Tel: 1800 654 013
www.acd.org.au
Information and support for children with
disabilities and their families.

NEW ZEALAND
DPA
Tel: 04 801 9100
www.dpa.org.nz
Advice and information for people with all kinds
of disabilities.

BOOKS
*Going Shopping: Meet Sara who uses a
Wheelchair*
Dianne Church, Franklin Watts 2003

Let's talk about being in a Wheelchair,
Melanie Apel Gordon, Powerkids Press 2003

What do we think about disability?
Jillian Powell, Hodder 1998